Stanza & Spice
…And everything nice
Vol 1

By Miko Black

PenFire Publishing

Penfire Publishing
Kansas City, MO
www.spokenpurpose.com/PenFirePublishing

Copyright © 2023
All rights reserved. No part of this book may be reproduced, scanned, or distributed in any printed or electronic form, including information storage and retrieval systems, without permission. Please do not participate in or encourage piracy of copyrighted materials in violation of the author's rights.

Please purchase only authorized editions.

First Edition: February 2023
ISBN: 978-1-952838-12-5

This book is a work of fiction. Names, characters, places, dates, and incidents are products of the author's imagination, or are used fictitiously, satirically, or as parody. Any resemblance to actual persons, living or dead, business establishments, events, or locales is entirely coincidental.

10 9 8 7 6 5 4 3 2 1

Design, Layout, Edits, Cover Art: Sheri Purpose Hall

Dedication

Every person who says, "I'm not used to hearing you speak like this." is a person who got comfortable with the portrait of you they built without indulging the possibility of more. Inside every human, there is a parent, a spouse, a firecracker, a shit starter, an advocate, a lover, a teacher, a prayer warrior, a jokester, a person who doesn't give a fuck, and a whore. We are holy miscreants, fleshly and divine.

This book is for everyone who feels they cannot embrace all parts of themselves. It is for every person who cannot find all those parts due to trauma. It is for every person who feels those parts have faded. It is for every person who felt like they couldn't say what they wanted to say, when, how, and to whom they wanted to say it. It is for those whose sexuality and opinionated tongue have been suppressed.

I assure you, it's still in you, and it is still you, just not the "you" they're used to.

Miko Black aka Shao aka Arsyn aka Blackie aka All Purpose … Sheri Purpose Hall
The
mother, lover, cheerleader, introvert, wild child, sister, nurturer, advocate, activist, mouthpiece, pinup, goofball, minister, peer, counselor, mentor, siren, servant, leader, teacher
…Poet

Table of Contents

~~A couple~~
~~Some~~
~~Most~~
ALL
of these poems are not suitable for children.
They break all structure rules
and contain profanity
and explicit content
Parental discretion is advised.

Plain English-
Don't you let yo kids read this damn book!

Dedication	iii
Anarchy Against Adulting	1
Body Count	4
How you … ?	7
Beard	9
Long Distance	11
Self-Care	13
Love Languages	15
Bio	19

Anarchy Against Adulting

Hi, I'm Sheri Purpose Hall, and today, I am the part of you that gets tired, irritated, or overworked and wants to say F U C K   I T !

Luckily for you, today is FUCK IT Day, otherwise known as Anarchy Against Adulting Day.

So,
FUCK all this shit!
Flip all this shit over!
Don't pay no bills,
    FUCK THEM BILLS.
Don't feed them kids,
    FUCK
(and I cannot emphasize this enough)
        THEM KIDS!
Them kids better fuck around
and learn how to fuckin live.
And when I say fuck them kids,
I mean the infant too.
Don't go to work,
    FUCK THAT JOB.
If you tha boss,
    FUCK THEM EMPLOYEES.
FUCK the cleaning and the chores.
FUCK all the people who
want you to give a fuck for fuckin free!
    FUCK THAT and FUCK THEM.
Tell them fuck moochin hoes
to get some fucks of they own.
I'm sure someone has fucks on clearance!

We not giving a FUCK today.
We gon do what the fuck we want.
We gon wash our ass when we feel like it

and when we do, we gon use
all the hot water and the good soap.
We gon air dry our nuts;
be butt naked on a balcony
drinking pumpkin spice;
wear white after Labor Day;
open umbrellas in the house;
jump on the furniture.
> FUCK YO COUCH
> NIGGA FUCK YO COUCH!

We eatin all the carbs and sugar.
*When's the last time you had
a French fry my guy?*
Eat that shit.
> FUCK IT!

We gon take long naps
in the middle of the afternoon,
and when we wake up
we gon fuck ourselves.
Having problems in your relationship?
> FUCK IT!

Fuck someone else.
Ladies,
if you ain't got no one in ya life,
walk past a mirror
and grab your own ass twice.
Men,
admit that you like your nipples licked,
and find someone to do that shit.
If they look at you crazy
drop that judgemental bitch!

And I mean that shit.
You deserve your nipples licked
just as much as you deserve to say
> FUCK IT.

And when I say I mean that shit,
I mean, I mean that shit.

Do all the things,
Do none of the things
    FUCK IT!

And yeah,
I know that Fuck It day
may earn some of us a life in prison
or land us in divorce court,
but never mind all that.
What matters is
for the last 3 minutes
you lived the dream,
And haven't thought seriously
about any of your responsibilities.
You had a moment of self-care.
So congratulations on saying
    FUCK IT,
Even for a little while.
And soon you will integrate
small parts of fuck it
into your lifestyle.

Because you need to,
because sometimes
we all need to say
    FUCK IT.

This message has been brought to you by the National Association of Adulting and Peopling Skills. Please celebrate Fuck It Day responsibly. Don't forget to stretch. Don't drink and drive. Use your seat belt. Wipe front to back. Wash behind your ears and under your nut sack. Remember, snitches, get stitches, and drink your Ovaltine.

Body Count

In response to the question
    "What's your number?"
I don't count bodies; I collect them.

The organ that has you worried is **experienced**. This **clitoris** has over 8000 nerve endings, can be stimulated from the outside and inside, **orgasms** multiple times, never ages. The more you use it, the better it gets, **sustains more wetness**. **It's** a self-cleaning thing; doesn't need your approval to make it saved, sanctified, or **Holy**. You will not use your filthy rag morality to judge me.

Pretend to be a high-value man, and I will ask you about the escort services where you currently use your currency.

I'm **not property, but** metaphorically speaking, are you asking how many people have lived in this house or how many passed through? *(As if a house that has had house parties has a devalued **value**.)* After all, my curbside **appeal** was enough to catch you.

It would be different if you wanted to know how many spirits I've entertained and soul ties I've attained instead of how many souls I snatched and wonder if I remember the names.

Are you trying to check my **standards**? After I tell you my number, you gon ask me:

        The median income of all of the men
      How many of them had college education
           Postgraduate degrees
           Where they worked
            Who they were
     How many had all their **original** teeth
            Dental implants

Cavities
Roth IRA's
401ks
Checking accounts
Credit cards
Hid money under the mattress?

Is this a fancy way of trying to see if they put money in my hand or on the nightstand? You wanna see if I got that **fire** or that killer? Wanna see if my lower lips have spoken eulogies? Wanna know if their fingernails were clipped or clean, Vegan, Christian, 5%? You wanna know what kind of soap they use and where I got that move?

I get it; you want me to be **experienced** enough to know what to do but not so experienced as to outdo you.
But I'll tell you what this **mouth** do.

I'm a truth teller; I even orgasm honest. You a bootleg scientist asking quantitative questions without qualitative analysis, and it all counts.

Long term relationships
Homies
One times

But if I told you that rape and molestation were also a part of this count, you'd try to diagnose presumed promiscuity. Imma save you the brain work, I do what the hell I want.

I've said yes with consent
Yes while coerced
Yes inebriated
Yes sober
I've said no and stayed
No and had to run
No and been punched
No in the presence of a gun

No and fought
I have said yes at times, even inside relationships,
Then grieved and was fully distraught.

And at the end of all this, you will still be more pissed about how many times I said **yes** than the times my **no** was ignored. You ain't even ask who or if I'm dealing with anyone right now, so what the fuck are you asking for?

But since you asked, I'm an OG at this.

My lips
        Have sucked the depression right up outta
Dick
        Stands at attention then bows before the Queen's
Hips
        Giving release and rejuvenation
Gripping
        Life-saving thighs
These breasts
        Have nurtured nations
My love
        Is **revolutionary**
                      I have **martyred** this pussy
                      So niggas could say they **killed** it.

I'm not a whore, ho, or sex worker, though it wouldn't matter if I was.

I am a healthy, disease-free, grown-assed, unattached, fine-assed woman. **I am a lover**, have had lovers, and was willing to consider you.

But it seems that's not what you're into, so a real conversation isn't due.

So as far as it concerns you,
                            I'm a virgin.

How you ... ?

How you fuck up fuckin?
A Senryu String

                I got a story
About when I dissa-damn-
           peared on a nigga

            He was a mellow,
cutie. Nice with the convo,
           surgeon with the tool

       He blew my back out,
then stalked me. Like huh? Why you
           being weird to me?

        I said, "Self." Me said,
"Huh?" I said, "Biiiiiiiitch, this nigga
           crazy! Ditch his ass!"

          He caught up to me,
but I ain't wanna converse.
       He begged, "Please tell me!"

         How you tell a man
he's too good? Stroke game crazy
          'n mouth ain't lazy.

       Same time he slick, a
bit secretive loves love but
           no relationship.

         Also, free pussy
only had one condition
      DO NOT LIE TO ME!

      I told him he got
hobosexual, empty
    your bank account, dick.

He got that play house
till he gets too into it
then jump ship, type dick.

He said, "I got a
good job and a crib." I said,
"That's irrelevant."

I ain't stupid. You
dangerous; act all nice, then
leave my heart vacant.

Buy me Roses but
want my thorns to dull. Nothing
left to save myself.

He said, "Save yourself?
From who, me?" I said, "No love,
to save me from me.

I've made enough bad
decisions that turn into
damn good poetry.

You are a muse a
crisp air, twilight bloodsucker,
love and leave me drained.

Instead of being
filled up after being with
you, I feel empty.

Depression flirts with
transference of energy
and low self-esteem.

I want you, but you've
got a nomad vampire
succubus spirit.

Inhabit my soul,
suck it dry, and leave nothing
but dirt and good dick

Companionship sans
the emotional labor
it takes to keep it.

Really tho, why you
chasing me, my guy? You said
no relationship."

He said, "Yeah but I
ain't no hit and quit. You got
that fye I'd stay with."

I said, "You just hate
situations where you can't
win. I'm not a game.

Play with yaself, not
with me. We did what we did;
we indeed agreed."

He said, "You a cold
piece." I said, "Not like you Young
Jeezy you Icy."

He said, "On the real
I could see myself with you."
I said, "Shiit shhhiiiiit shiiiitttt!"

He shrugged me off, then
called another bitch, been with
her over three years.

He was also still
seeing his baby momma
and lying to me.

The moral of the
story is protect your peace,
give him his release.

And don't answer the
phone, D Ms, or the door when
you dis-a-damn-pear.

Beard

There's nothing quite like the scent of pussy juice in hair, especially when I put it there. I bless your face overflowing, quiver, shake. Your face becomes a water tower I write my name on with hip swivels.

        And you are an oddity!
        Are you mammal or fish?
        You under, still breathing?
        Do you got gills?
        You a whale at this!

Scaled movement measurements; you skilled at this! Swear to GAWD, this tongue feels like it's drawing Disney animation on my clitoris –
        "Unda da sea.
        Darling it's betta
        Down where it's wetta"
                Fuck the alphabet.

But when you come up for air with my cum in your hair,

        Your beard becomes incense.
I suck your chin scent less; eat me off you; inhale your face emaciated; suck your tongue as if to remove my delectable
        from your buds to create a clean slate.
Start over.
Travel back down for more nourishment. Your countenance cradled by lips, tongue slides electric. SHOCKING. You clutch my pearl; I gasp, then sing. A sweet melody hitting every note with precision.
        Your neck is a
        Stevie Wonder tribute
        Ribbon in my thighs,
        Wanye wind
        With hips locked in arms
        Gripping stomach with fingertips

            Out bodies together in a jam session
                Hopping and jiving
                Under your direction
And we just can't stop dancing, grooving.

                We hold hands tight.
                        change tempo
                        slow grind
                        speed up
                Still holding hands.
                        inhale
                        breathe deeply
                Still holding hands.
                        fingers interlocked
                You refuse to let me go.
                I refuse to let go.
You make me release,   And release,   And release.

You mathematician, teach me multiples, exponents,
Pythagoras in my triangle. A squared plus B squared
makes me see squared.
                                        I mean double.
                I mean, my eyes rolled,
                        And crossed,
                        And closed,
                        And I can't move,
                        And I'm high,
And this head gave me cotton mouth, my mouth dry.
You smirk, coming up to my face with
THAT DAMN BEARD!
                Dripping of me and you,
                        And juice
                        And sweat
                        And wet
        And I can't think to do nuthin' but
                                        Drink.

Long Distance

I miss you. I hate being so far away from you that I can't put my hands on you, so you put your hands on you.

Record.
Video chat.
Lemme see it.
I enjoy your enjoyment.

Lemme talk you through it. Remind you what a mind fuck I am. I give good brain.

Role play.
Lemme be your only fan.
I Cashapp you at the end.

We play show and tell. I tell you, my tongue can reach my nipple and draw circles 'round my areola. You tell me you wanna see. I show tongue flips, and you reminisce. I tell you, I miss
        E v e r y   i n c h   o f   i t .

While you watch me make my cocoa caramel glisten with the same spit that wets your bed, I'm messy.

Screenshot.
Screen record.
Lemme see you stroke.

Lemme see you play on the edge.
You edge, closer and closer;
Hold it,
Grip.
Not yet.

I got time today.

Lemme hear you. Those sounds you make while stimulating the head, fingers on frenulum, attempting to mimic my fierce tongue lashing. Lemme talk shit to that dick. You make it obedient. Beat it till it does what I tell it, and it betta do what I tell it.

Stand when I say.
Cum when I say.
It jerks so much it talks back. You moan back to back.
Stutters so much I can't even understand what you sayin'.

Cum again?

You are a natural wonder, a geyser exploding from the base, a fountain erupting beautifully.

    D o n ' t   d r o p   t h a t   p h o n e .

Hold it up. I wanna see it finish all the way.

    D o n ' t   s t o p .

You breathe deep, recover.
You say
    I'm glad I called
I say
    I'm glad you came. Save the rest till we meet again.

Self-Care

Fuck self-care.

Don't speak the self-care gospel to me like it's new. I said what I said.

F u c k self-care.

Everyone says,
 Self-care, sis, self-care. Have you done self-care?

Self-care, like it's a magical fixer.

Like I ain't
- been taking care of myself all this damn time.
- cut off toxic relationships,
- prayed, meditated, fasted, read books, and exercised this whole damn time.
- managed my own triggers; ain't pulled no triggers.
- been going through my struggles sober and wide-eyed.
- been in recovery this whole damn time.

Like
- taking care of oneself isn't work within itself.
- planning a vacation isn't stressful in and of itself.
- figuring out what to do or what not to do ain't fuckin' traumatic.

No, Fuck that!

You see me drowning
and flailing in the waters,
you take care of me.
Black girl magic, my ass!

Take care of me.

Offer the massage
Offer the meal
Offer the chocolate
Anything

Without Dick Attached!

Unless … that's what I want.

							In which case,
					lay pipe Mario and bring Luigi.
	I mean, workshop me.
			Mix my drinks, alcoholic or non.
			Feed me or respect when I don't want to eat.
Help me.
			Clean my house.
			Hug my children for me.
		Do the necessary without me opening my mouth.
		You see me struggling, do something about it!
Send me on vacation with spending money.
Find a way to appreciate me and leave it at that
without shouting to the hills that you *Did That.*

				Or maybe, just love me.
				| without paying rent on time spent
Let me vent | without offering all these damn suggestions
				| trying to sound like you have the answers,
				| wading through rebuttal after rebuttal of mine

	Maybe, I don't want to think of a solution this time.
		Maybe, all of this is too much.

		| just let it be too much for me right now?
		| agree and say you understand what I'm feeling?
		| remind me that what I'm feeling is a human experience?
Can you | tell me I'm worth it?
		| respond to me like I'm worth it?
		| say what needs saying and mean it?
		| ask me what's on my mind
		| and be a safe space for me to release it?
		| sit in silence with me?
		| hold space for me?

				Can you care for me?
				Because right now,
			I can't for myself.

Love Languages

as it pertains to love languages
i'm an
>acts of service
>physical touch
>quality time

kinda girl
oddly almost even in the categories
i give like i receive
i give all of me
and for you to feel my love
i can't just say it with my chest
it has to be deep throat
pipe down my windpipe
lungs filled with precum

fellatio

an act of service
requiring physical touch
and quality time
my mouth is a love language

a toasty caress
wet with devotion
saturating length and girth
my love is
>a lake current

engulfing head
shaft
tongue told
your twin friends
to come in
I take all of you
>*hard or soft*

i lick chest
kiss stomach while it's

sandwiched between breasts
bite inner thigh
work the body like a coach
my tongue laps run laps
around your lap like a track
i'm an olympian with five rings
and you're a champ peen
i endure to the finish
swallow the spoils of victory
    i'm an addict

my love language may be
    acts of service
but i have selfish needs
    i'm a voyeur
your pleasure is my silver screen
i watch
    you
watch me
increase intensity
we play stare down and i win
as you let your head fall back

    i make you white man relax
    without a care in the world
a state of ease
your hand grips my hair
trapped in my locs and curls
controls my neck a lil bit
chest rise and fall
and bite your lip
back of tongue
front of tongue
lick and switch
my tongue is a wand
and i do magic
make it rise
jerk
the vein throbs

the manly moan that escapes
it's the only noise taking place
over the splosh of suck juice

a river wet wet flowing
cheek to lips
running
dripping
into every crevasse
giving skin to skin
slick nourishment
my love is a moisturizer
and i treat your whole dermis

massage it firmly
rub you the right way
for every time
        you were wronged
make your eyes roll
for every time
        you were dismissed
make your toes curl
for every
        step you took today
for every
        gawk and glare
i gawk with care

i love you
till you know you're important enough
to have time spent like this

my love language is
        oral encouragement
and i will
        receive you
        welcome you
        want you
        please you
no matter how long It takes

Bio

Stanza and Spice is the first installment and project from the new author Miko Black. Miko is an honest-hearted free spirit with an intense love for words. Her fiery "take no mess" attitude is executed through her writing style and performance. She is known for telling it like it is with sass yet still exuding sultry feminine confidence. She has worked in the background with many groups and authors, including the Regulators, Poetry for Personal Power, East of Red ArtHouse, and many community organizations. She encourages women to walk in their entire identities and believes that women's empowerment is women actively taking a front seat in the representation of their complete sphere. Miko states, "The only way to receive holistic care is for women to bring their whole selves to the table, unashamed. Walk in your full identity."

For more info email mikoblack777@gmail.com